The White House
February 4, 2011

Declaration by President Obama and Prime Minister Harper of Canada

Beyond the Border:
A Shared Vision for Perimeter Security and Economic Competitiveness

The United States and Canada are staunch allies, vital economic partners, and steadfast friends. We share common values, deep links among our citizens, and deeply rooted ties. The extensive mobility of people, goods, capital, and information between our two countries has helped ensure that our societies remain open, democratic, and prosperous.

To preserve and extend the benefits our close relationship has helped bring to Americans and Canadians alike, we intend to pursue a perimeter approach to security, working together within, at, and away from the borders of our two countries to enhance our security and accelerate the legitimate flow of people, goods, and services between our two countries. We intend to do so in partnership, and in ways that support economic competitiveness, job creation, and prosperity.

We have advanced our prosperity through the *U.S.–Canada Free Trade Agreement and the North American Free Trade Agreement*. Over $250 billion of direct investment by each country in the other, and bilateral trade of more than half-a-trillion dollars a year in goods and services create and sustain millions of jobs in both our countries. At the U.S.–Canada border, nearly one million dollars in goods and services cross every minute, as well as 300,000 people every day, who cross for business, pleasure, or to maintain family ties.

The United States and Canada share a long history of cooperation in defending our values and freedoms. We stand together to confront threats to our collective security as partners in the North Atlantic Treaty Organization. We work shoulder-to-shoulder in the defense of both our nations through the North American Aerospace Defense Command (NORAD).

We share responsibility for the safety, security, and resilience of the United States and of Canada in an increasingly integrated and globalized world. We intend to address security threats at the earliest point possible in a manner that respects privacy, civil liberties, and human rights.

I. Principles

We intend to work together in cooperation and partnership to develop, implement, manage, and monitor security initiatives, standards, and practices to fulfill our vision. We recognize that our efforts should accelerate job creation and economic growth through trade facilitation at our borders and contribute directly to the economic security and well-being of both the United States and Canada.

We intend to strengthen our resilience—our ability to mitigate, respond to, and recover from disruptions. Success depends on readiness at all levels of our governments, within our communities, and among private sector owners and operators of our infrastructure, systems, and networks. We rely on secure communications and transportation networks, including our civil aviation system, and we intend to work together to make them resilient enough to continue operating in the face of a natural disaster or attack.

We expect to use a risk management approach where compatible, interoperable, and—where possible—joint measures and technology should proportionately and effectively address the threats we share. Effective risk management should enable us to accelerate legitimate flows of people and goods into the United States and Canada and across our common border, while enhancing the physical security and economic competitiveness of our countries.

We build on the efforts of many partners—from police and other emergency workers to our armed forces—who continue to safeguard us from the complex threats we face.

We also recognize that cooperation across air, land, and maritime domains, as well as in space and cyberspace, our enduring bi-national defense relationship, and military support for civilian authorities engaged in disaster response efforts and critical infrastructure protection, have all contributed significantly to the security of our populations.

We recognize that greater sharing of information will strengthen our ability to achieve the goals of this vision.

We intend to work together to engage with all levels of government and with communities, non-governmental organizations, and the private sector, as well as with our citizens, on innovative approaches to security and competitiveness.

We value and respect our separate constitutional and legal frameworks that protect privacy, civil liberties, and human rights and provide for appropriate recourse and redress.

We recognize the sovereign right of each country to act independently in its own interest and in accordance with its laws.

We expect to work together with third countries and with international organizations, and intend to facilitate security sector reform and capacity building around the globe, to enhance standards that contribute to our overall security.

Key Areas of Cooperation

Addressing Threats Early
Collaborating to address threats before they reach our shores, we expect to develop a common understanding of the threat environment through improved intelligence and information sharing, as well as joint threat assessments to support informed risk management decisions.

We intend to develop an integrated strategy that would enable us to meet the threats and hazards that both our nations face, including natural disasters and man-made threats, including terrorism.

We expect to continue strengthening our health security partnership, through existing mechanisms for cooperation on health emergencies, and by further enhancing our collective preparedness and response capacity to a range of health security threats, including influenza pandemics.

We intend to work together to uncover and disrupt threats that endanger the security of both the United States and Canada and to establish those agreements or policies necessary to ensure timely sharing of information for combined efforts to counter the threats. We intend to ensure we have the ability to support one another as we prepare for, withstand, and rapidly recover from disruptions. We intend to make the *Agreement Between the Government of the United States of America and the Government of Canada on Emergency Management Cooperation,* updated in 2008, a cornerstone of these efforts.

To increase security, counter fraud, and improve efficiency, we intend to work together to establish and verify the identities of travelers and conduct screening at the earliest possible opportunity. We intend to work toward common technical standards for the collection, transmission, and matching of biometrics that enable the sharing of information on travelers in real time. This collaboration should facilitate combined United States and Canadian screening efforts and strengthen methods of threat notification.

In order to promote mobility between our two countries, we expect to work towards an integrated United States–Canada entry-exit system, including work towards the exchange of relevant entry information in the land environment so that documented entry into one country serves to verify exit from the other country.

We intend to cooperate to identify, prevent, and counter violent extremism in our two countries. By working cooperatively on research, sharing best practices, and emphasizing community-based and community-driven efforts, we will have a better understanding of this threat and an increased ability to address it effectively.

We intend to formulate jointly United States–Canada privacy protection principles that should inform and guide our work in relation to facilities, operations, programs, and other initiatives contemplated by this Declaration.

We intend to work together to promote the principles of human rights, privacy, and civil liberties as essential to the rule of law and effective management of our perimeter.

Trade Facilitation, Economic Growth, and Jobs
We intend to pursue creative and effective solutions to manage the flow of traffic between the United States and Canada. We will focus investment in modern infrastructure and technology at our busiest land ports of entry, which are essential to our economic well-being.

We will strive to ensure that our border crossings have the capacity to support the volume of commercial and passenger traffic inherent to economic growth and job creation on both sides of the border.

To enhance our risk management practices, we intend to continue planning together, organizing bi-national port of entry committees to coordinate planning and funding, building, expanding or modernizing shared border management facilities and border infrastructure where appropriate, and using information technology solutions.

We intend to look for opportunities to integrate our efforts and where practicable, to work together to develop joint facilities and programs—within and beyond the United States and Canada—to increase efficiency and effectiveness for both security and trade.

We aim to build on the success of current joint programs by expanding trusted traveler and trader programs, harmonizing existing programs, and automating processes at the land border to increase efficiency.

We will look for ways to reduce the cost of conducting legitimate business across the border by implementing, where practicable, common practices and streamlined procedures for customs processing and regulatory compliance.

We intend to work towards developing an integrated cargo security strategy that ensures compatible screening methods for goods and cargo before they depart foreign ports bound for the United States or Canada, so that once they enter the territory of either we can, together, accelerate subsequent crossings at land ports of entry between our two countries.

We recognize the importance of the *U.S.–Canada Framework for the movement of Goods and People across the Border During and Following an Emergency,* agreed to in 2009. It underscores the importance of coordinated, cooperative, and timely border management decision making to mitigate the impacts of disruptions on our citizens and economies.

Integrated Cross-border Law Enforcement

We intend to build on existing bilateral law enforcement programs to develop the next generation of integrated cross-border law enforcement operations that leverage cross-designated officers and resources to jointly identify, assess, and interdict persons and organizations involved in transnational crime.

We intend to seek further opportunities to pursue national security and transnational crime investigations together to maximize our ability to tackle the serious security threats that these organizations and individuals present.

We intend to improve the sharing among our law enforcement agencies of relevant information to better identify serious offenders and violent criminals on both sides of the border.

Critical Infrastructure and Cybersecurity

We intend to work together to prevent, respond to, and recover from physical and cyber disruptions of critical infrastructure and to implement a comprehensive cross-border approach to strengthen the resilience of our critical and cyber infrastructure with strong cross-border engagement.

The United States and Canada benefit from shared critical and cyber infrastructure. Our countries intend to strengthen cybersecurity to protect vital government and critical digital infrastructure of national importance, and to make cyberspace safer for all our citizens.

We intend to work together to defend and protect our use of air, land, sea, space, and cyberspace, and enhance the security of our integrated transportation and communications networks.

II. Implementation and Oversight

The United States and Canada intend to establish a Beyond the Border Working Group (BBWG) composed of representatives from the appropriate departments and offices of our respective federal governments.

Responsibility for ensuring inter-agency coordination will rest with the President and the Prime Minister and their respective officials.

We intend for the BBWG to report to their respective Leaders in the coming months, and after a period of consultation, with a joint Plan of Action to realize the goals of this declaration, that would, where appropriate, rely upon existing bilateral border-related groups, for implementation.

The BBWG will report on the implementation of this declaration to Leaders on an annual basis. The mandate of the BBWG will be reviewed after three years.

Table of Contents

Beyond the Border:
A Shared Vision for Perimeter Security and Economic Competiveness

Action Plan

On February 4, 2011, the Prime Minister of Canada and the President of the United States issued *Beyond the Border: A Shared Vision for Perimeter Security and Economic Competitiveness*. The Declaration established a new long-term partnership built upon a perimeter approach to security and economic competitiveness. This means working together, not just at the border, but "beyond the border" to enhance our security and accelerate the legitimate flow of people, goods, and services. Leaders called for the development of a joint Action Plan to realize this goal, which is embodied in this document.

This Action Plan sets out joint priorities for achieving that vision within the four areas of cooperation identified in the Beyond the Border Declaration: addressing threats early; trade facilitation, economic growth, and jobs; cross-border law enforcement; and critical infrastructure and cyber security. Nothing in this Action Plan is intended to give rise to rights or obligations under domestic or international law; this action plan is not intended to constitute an international treaty under international law. Work to implement this Action Plan will be subject to normal budget, legal, and regulatory mechanisms in each country and will be carried out in close consultation with interested stakeholders in both countries. In particular, progress on many of the elements of this Action Plan will depend on the availability of funding. In those cases, appropriations to support implementation will be sought through the normal budgetary processes of each country.

In addition to calling for this Action Plan, the Declaration of Leaders on February 4, 2011, also created a Canada–United States Regulatory Cooperation Council (RCC). Whereas this Action Plan aims to enhance security and economic competitiveness through measures taken at our shared perimeter and border, the RCC aims to better align our regulatory approaches to protect health, safety, and the environment while supporting growth, investment, innovation, and market openness. Some initiatives under this Action Plan will complement the work of the RCC, and indeed, could provide beneficial interim measures pending more fundamental regulatory solutions which may flow from the RCC.

Part I: Addressing Threats Early

Addressing threats at the earliest possible point is essential to strengthen the shared security of our countries and to enable us to improve the free flow of legitimate goods and people across the Canada–United States border. The Beyond the Border Action Plan will support this goal by developing a common understanding of the threat environment; aligning and coordinating our security systems for goods, cargo, and baggage; and supporting the effective identification of people who pose a threat, which will enhance safety and facilitate the movement of legitimate travelers.

Develop a Common Approach to Assessing Threats and Identifying Those Who Pose a Risk Under the Principle that a Threat to Either Country Represents a Threat to Both

- **Enhance our shared understanding of the threat environment through joint, integrated threat assessments, improving our intelligence and national security information sharing.**

  Next Steps: A bilateral group of senior government leaders with intelligence and public safety responsibilities will survey existing intelligence work to identify redundancies and gaps to develop a framework to guide the selection of joint projects. The framework will leverage existing forums, emphasize the need to economize resources, and establish performance metrics.

  Measuring Progress: The U.S. Office of the Director of National Intelligence, the U.S. Department of Homeland Security (DHS), and Public Safety Canada, in coordination with relevant intelligence agencies in both countries, will produce a joint inventory of existing intelligence work and a gap analysis and identify next steps by September 30, 2012.

- **Share information and intelligence in support of law enforcement and national security.**

  Next Steps: We will improve information sharing while respecting each country's respective constitutional and legal frameworks, including the following areas of work:

    - Addressing agency policies that may improve information sharing, including by developing clear channels or mechanisms for cross-border sharing of intelligence and information;

    - Promoting increased informal sharing of law enforcement intelligence, information, and evidence through police and prosecutorial channels consistent with the respective domestic laws of each country; and

    - Examining whether current frameworks should be changed to address impediments to cooperation, and to ensure that the terms of applicable laws, agreements and treaties provide the widest measure of cooperation possible.

We will utilize the Cross-Border Crime Forum and create other forums to discuss ways to improve law enforcement information sharing practices, and to identify opportunities to improve effective and responsible national security intelligence information sharing.

Measuring Progress: By January 31, 2012, the U.S. Department of Justice (DOJ), DHS, Public Safety Canada, and Justice Canada will determine the way ahead.

- **Enhance domain awareness in the air, land, and maritime environments.**

  Next Steps: We will develop and implement processes, procedures, and policies to enable an effective, shared understanding of activities, threats, and criminal trends or other consequences in the air, land, and maritime environments. This will be achieved through intelligence analysis, effective and timely information sharing, a common understanding of the environment, and an inventory of current capabilities. We will:

  - Create an inventory of American and Canadian domain awareness capabilities at the border by May 31, 2012, and identify gaps and vulnerabilities in capabilities by October 31, 2012;

  - Prioritize coverage of gaps by April 30, 2013, to create a vision for jointly deploying new technology to address identified gaps; and

  - Establish a process by April 30, 2013, to coordinate the joint procurement and deployment of technology along the border.

  Measuring Progress: DHS, the Royal Canadian Mounted Police (RCMP), and Transport Canada will report on progress toward achieving this work by the timelines indicated above.

- **Cooperate to counter violent extremism in our two countries.**

  Next Steps: We will:

  - Coordinate and share research on how people become radicalized and turn to violence;

  - Share best practices and tools for law enforcement and corrections partners to detect, prevent, and respond to this threat;

  - Develop a common messaging and strategic communications approach; and

  - Emphasize community-based and community-driven efforts. This will include collaborating on how to engage with communities and build their resilience against violent extremists who seek to target specific communities in our respective countries, as well as coordinating community outreach.

  Measuring Progress: Progress updates will be provided to the U.S. Secretary of Homeland Security and Canadian Minister of Public Safety on a semi-annual basis.

Pushing Out the Border: Stopping Threats Before they Arrive in Either the United States or Canada

- **Develop a harmonized approach to screening inbound cargo arriving from offshore that will result in increased security and the expedited movement of secure cargo across the United States–Canada border, under the principle of "cleared once, accepted twice."**

  Next Steps: We will develop an integrated, multi-modal customs and transportation security regime, which will reduce duplication and move activities away from the United States–Canada border. This regime will enhance the security of supply chains, starting at the earliest possible point in the supply chain and ensuring the integrity of the "screened" cargo through to its destination. Both countries will make better informed risk-management decisions due to advanced information sharing for inbound offshore cargo shipments, harmonization of advance data requirements, sharing of real time pre-load screening and examination results, and the harmonization of targeting and risk assessment methodologies and results that are key elements to the success of this initiative.

  The initiative will build on previous agreements and existing programs of work. The work will include mutual recognition of air cargo systems, the integration of advance data requirements for advanced security screening, and finally, a joint strategy to address security risks associated with inbound shipments from offshore.

  Mutual Recognition of Air Cargo: We will evaluate and achieve mutual recognition of our respective air cargo security programs for passenger aircraft by March 2012. We will ensure that there is a commensurate set of security controls so that both countries' programs achieve equivalent levels of security to eliminate rescreening except for cause.

  Advance Data Requirements: We also agree by June 30, 2012, to develop a common set of required data elements for all modes of transport for advance security screening of cargo, including the targeted populations for collections, timing for collections, and what data elements are needed as a common set of elements for collection. We will:

  - Develop common sets of data elements required for in-bond (United States) /in-transit (Canada) shipments arriving from offshore, and for domestic shipments which transit through the other country. We will limit the data sets required to those necessary for effective, risk-based enforcement.

  - Identify and evaluate options by September 2012 under which trusted traders could use alternate processes and approaches to submit advance data elements, including examining whether and how, existing program flexibilities can be enhanced.

  - Implement by December 2013 the common sets of required data, as well as any alternate processes and approaches for trusted traders.

  Integrated Cargo Security Strategy (ICSS): The United States and Canada will develop a joint strategy to address risks associated with shipments arriving from offshore based on informed risk management. This strategy is aimed at identifying and resolving security and contraband concerns as early as possible in the supply chain or at the perimeter, with the expectation that this will allow us to reduce the level of these activities at the United States–Canada border. Over time, we will work to cover additional areas of activity, outside of the traditional security and contraband arena.

This initiative will proceed in two phases:

In Phase I, by June 30, 2012, we will develop the ICSS. The ICSS will address security risks associated with inbound shipments from offshore and lead to expedited crossings at the land border.

Phase II will begin with the launch of pilots in September 2012, which are intended to validate and shape the implementation of the strategy. We anticipate the implementation of the strategy will begin in 2014. Pilots will include targeted risk assessment for security and contraband.*

- Canada's pilots will be: Canada Border Security Agency (CBSA)-Transport Canada Cargo Targeting Initiative involving pre-load information and targeting in the air mode; perimeter vetting and examination of inbound marine cargo at Prince Rupert destined for Chicago by rail and of marine cargo arriving at Montreal destined to the United States by truck.

- U.S. pilots will involve the harmonization of targeting and risk assessment methodologies and the targeting and risk assessment of cargo arriving from offshore at a major U.S. port destined for Canada; and the testing of a new in-bond module for processing in-transit/in-bond (Canada–United States–Canada) cargo traveling by truck.

In support of this initiative, Canada will build new cargo examination facilities in Halifax and Vancouver, as required.

* Depending on the results of the study on wood packaging material, being carried out under the Pre-clearance and Pre-inspection Action Item, inspections of such material at the perimeter could be included in the ICSS.

Measuring Progress: DHS and Transport Canada will measure progress by:

- Mutual Recognition of Air Cargo: We expect to reduce the number of air cargo loads rescreened to zero beginning in March 2012.

- Advance Data Requirements: We will produce a common set of manifest data elements by June 2012 and implement it by December 2013.

- Integrated Cargo Security Strategy: We anticipate achieving a clear reduction in the number and volume of transshipments subjected to reinspection at the border on an annual basis, using 2011 as a baseline year.

- **Mutually recognize passenger baggage screening, as new technology is deployed and implemented.**

Next Steps: Canada will begin the deployment of Transportation Security Administration (TSA) Explosive Detection Systems (EDS) certified equipment at preclearance airports immediately and will seek to complete the deployment by March 31, 2015. Concurrently, the United States will lift the rescreening requirement on an airport-by-airport basis for U.S. connecting checked baggage as each preclearance airport completes implementation of TSA-certified EDS.

Measuring Progress: TSA and Transport Canada will report on EDS deployment milestones and lifting of the rescreening requirement as determined by Transport Canada's rollout schedule of TSA-certified equipment at preclearance airports. TSA and Transport Canada also will measure the success through reporting of cost savings to air carriers realized from eliminating rescreening, as well as the reduction in Canadian originating baggage that misconnects in U.S. locations.

- **Better protect the United States and Canada from offshore food safety and animal and plant health risks by conducting joint assessments and audits for plant, animal, and food safety systems in third countries.**

Next Steps: With respect to animals and plants, we will:

- Develop, by December 31, 2012, assessment processes and joint site visit plans for commodities of common interest from third countries and address how to incorporate the findings of these site visits into risk management decisions; and

- Develop a mechanism to share the results of assessments when conducted separately.

With respect to food safety systems, by December 31, 2012, we will:

- Develop joint methodologies, including audit criteria, for conducting audits;

- Develop joint audit plans to pilot the evaluation of foreign food safety inspection systems in third countries, the outcomes of which will be used to establish the protocol and a plan for future joint audits; and

- Develop a protocol for what information from audits can be shared, how it may be shared, and how to use the findings of these site visits in risk management decisions.

Measuring Progress: Animal and Plant Health Inspection Service (APHIS), Food Safety and Inspection Service (FSIS), and the Canadian Food Inspection Agency (CFIA) will report on progress toward achieving this work by the timelines indicated above.

Establish a Common Approach to Perimeter Screening to Promote Security and Border Efficiency

The United States and Canada will screen travelers seeking to enter either country in order to:

- At the earliest point possible, identify individuals who seek to enter the perimeter for *mala fide* purposes and prevent them from traveling to the United States or Canada;

- Prevent individuals from assuming different identities between one country and the other;

- Identify those who have committed serious crimes or violated immigration law in the other country and enable informed decisions on visas, admissibility, or other immigration benefits; and

- Create a shared responsibility between the United States and Canada concerning those entering the perimeter, while facilitating ongoing efforts to streamline procedures at the United States–Canada border, thereby promoting trade and travel.

In order to accomplish these goals, the United States and Canada will:

- Use a **common approach to screening** methodologies and programs, including pre-travel screening and targeting; "board/no-board" perimeter screening and decision processes, and technology;

- Share **relevant, reliable, and accurate** information within the legal and privacy regimes of both countries, such as information contained on biographic and biometric national security watchlists, certain traveler criminal history records, and immigration violations; and

- Share United States–Canada entry data at the land border such that the **entry information from one country could constitute the exit information** from another through an integrated entry and exit system.

In achieving this approach, the United States and Canada will respect each other's sovereignty. Each country will maintain its right to independent decisionmaking and risk assessment as well as its independent databases. The United States and Canada do not intend to enforce each others' laws; instead, the intent is to share information to enable each country to have better information to enforce and administer its own laws.

- **Establishing a common approach to screening travelers.**

  Next Steps: We commit to implement an enhanced approach to identifying and interdicting inadmissible persons at the perimeter. To initiate a shift in this direction, Canada will implement two initiatives over the next 4 years: the Electronic Travel Authorization (eTA), to improve screening of all visa-exempt foreign nationals, and Interactive Advance Passenger Information (IAPI) to make "board or no-board" decisions on all travelers flying to Canada prior to departure. These initiatives will mirror measures taken in the United States through its Electronic System for Travel Authorization (ESTA) and Advance Passenger Information System Quick Query systems. Canada also will implement an enhanced, scenario-based passenger targeting methodology, consistent with the U.S. methodology, by October 2013. Consistent with existing bilateral information sharing agreements, the United States and Canada will share information about certain individuals, such as those denied boarding or entry as a result of national security concerns.

  Measuring Progress: Canada will join the United States in tracking performance indicators such as: the number of inadmissible persons denied permission to travel; the number of high-risk targets identified; and the number of subsequent enforcement actions taken that were facilitated by targeting.

- **Share relevant information to improve immigration and border determinations, establish and verify the identities of travelers, and conduct screening at the earliest possible opportunity.**

  Next Steps: We will:

  - Share risk assessment/targeting scenarios, and enhance real time notifications regarding the arrival of individuals on U.S. security watchlists;

  - Provide access to information on those who have been removed or who have been refused admission or a visa from either country, as well as those who have been removed from their respective countries for criminal reasons; and

  - Implement a systematic and automated biographic information sharing capability by 2013 and biometric information sharing capability by 2014 to reduce identity fraud and enhance screening decisions, and in support of other administrative and enforcement actions.

  We also will explore opportunities to broaden asylum cooperation to address irregular migration flows. Working groups will be tasked with developing proposals for practical cooperation, reporting back within 12 months.

  Measuring Progress: DHS, Citizenship and Immigration Canada, and the Canada Border Services Agency will assess the results of bilateral information sharing. Specifically, each country will:

  - Review the number of exchanges from which information was provided to visa, immigration and border control decisionmakers before they made a decision;

  - Monitor and report on match rates and the use of information obtained in refugee claim adjudication in respective asylum systems; and

  - Track the results of bilateral biometric-based information sharing, specifically: the number of queries sent and percent of total application volume; the number and percent of matches; the number of cases of identity fraud detected; and the number of exchanges where information was provided to immigration and border control decisionmakers before they made a decision.

- **Establish and coordinate entry and exit information systems, including a system which permits sharing information so that the record of a land entry into one country can be utilized to establish an exit record from the other.**

    Next Steps: To establish coordinated entry and exit systems at the common land border, we commit to develop a system to exchange biographical information on the entry of travelers, including citizens, permanent residents, and third country nationals, such that a record of entry into one country could be considered as a record of an exit from the other. Implementation will be phased in:

    – By September 30, 2012, we will begin implementation of a pilot project exchanging the data of third country nationals, permanent residents of Canada, and lawful permanent residents in the United States, at 2 to 4 automated common land border ports of entry;

    – By June 30, 2013, we will begin implementation of a program exchanging the data of third country nationals, permanent residents of Canada, and lawful permanent residents in the United States at all automated common land border ports of entry; and

    – By June 30, 2014, we will expand the program to include the exchange of data on all travelers at all automated common land border ports of entry.

    With respect to air travel, by June 30, 2014, Canada will develop a system to establish exit, similar to that in the United States, under which airlines will be required to submit their passenger manifest information on outbound international flights. Exploratory work will be conducted for future integration of entry and exit information systems for the marine and rail modes. The United States and Canada will share appropriate entry and exit information in these other modes in order to achieve our goals as set out in this Action Plan.

    Measuring Progress: DHS, Citizenship and Immigration Canada, and the Canada Border Services Agency will measure the security benefits of exit measures via the identification of: persons detected overstaying their visa and immigration warrant closures; entry and exit records matched that indicate a lawful exit from either country; individuals who may have failed to meet residency requirements for permanent resident status or citizenship applications; and persons subject to a removal or departure order and who are recorded as having departed.

Part II: Trade Facilitation, Economic Growth, and Jobs

The free flow of goods and services between the United States and Canada creates immense economic benefits for both countries. As our two countries work to strengthen the security of our shared perimeter, we will take steps simultaneously to create more openness at the land border for legitimate travel and trade. The Beyond the Border Action Plan enhances the benefits of programs that help trusted businesses and travelers move efficiently across the border; introduces new measures to facilitate movement and trade across the border while reducing the administrative burden for business; and invests in improvements to our shared border infrastructure and technology.

Enhance the Benefits of Programs that Help Trusted Businesses and Travelers Move Efficiently Across the Border

- **Adopt a common framework for trusted trader programs that will align requirements, enhance member benefits, and provide applicants with the opportunity to submit one application to multiple programs.**

  Next Steps: The United States and Canada will adopt a common framework for trusted trader programs that will align requirements, enhance member benefits and provide applicants with the opportunity to submit one application to multiple programs. Tier one will focus on supply chain security and tier two will focus on trade compliance and expedited border and accounting processes.

  Under tier one, we will:

    – Harmonize the U.S.-based Customs-Trade Partnership Against Terrorism (C-TPAT) program and the Canada-based Partners in Protection (PIP) program and offer new benefits, including an automated enrolment system. Canada will develop an interoperable communication portal similar to the United States' by December 2013.

    – Extend Free and Secure Trade (FAST) benefits to members in these programs at agreed locations beginning in mid-2012.

  With respect to tier two, we recognize that many trusted traders have invested significantly in supply chain security and have strong compliance records. We also recognize as fundamental that border agencies need advance information about shipments to conduct risk-based targeting. There are many ways to collect that information; therefore, we will:

    – Align Canada's Customs Self Assessment (CSA) and the U.S. Importer Self Assessment (ISA) programs to the greatest extent possible, while enabling members the flexibility to select the benefits that meet their business needs, and extend new benefits to tier-two members, such as expedited border and accounting processes and further reductions in risk-based examination rates. Canada will fully implement its Partners in Compliance (PIC) program by September 2012.

– Conduct a detailed comparison and review of CSA and ISA by June 2012, following which the United States will identify and provide expedited border processes and modernized, streamlined accounting processes to tier-two members.

– Jointly consult with tier-two stakeholders in both countries to identify and assess additional ways to expedite border processes. Recognizing that tier-two members have already provided us with extensive information, we will identify and assess options to collect data in advance through streamlined and more efficient means that are more responsive to shippers' business processes, while safeguarding our ability to assess individual shipments for the risk they may present. A report with recommendations on pilots or new initiatives will be completed and distributed to members by September 2012.

– Extend membership in these self-assessment programs to "non-resident importers" between the United States and Canada.

Canada will initiate a 1-year pilot to provide tier-two benefits to the processed-food sector by July 2012, which will enable participants to provide transactional data post-border to the regulatory authority and permit access to expedited clearance processes and lanes at the border in Canada. Within 1 year of the pilot's successful completion, permanent access to these program benefits will be provided to all approved companies by Canada.

In addition, we will explore product specific pilots aimed at lowering inspection rates for certain industry sectors based on regulatory compliance history. Canada will lead a pilot in the agri-food sector and the United States will lead a pilot in the pharmaceutical sector.

Measuring Progress: DHS and CBSA will measure the increased membership in trusted trader programs, the associated increased volume of trade covered by the programs, and lower examination rates and processing times for members. We will assess the success of the pilots discussed, above, and whether they have expedited trade.

- **Increase harmonized benefits to NEXUS members.**

  Next Steps: We will increase recognition and use of the existing binational NEXUS program to advance the risk-based screening approach in aviation and border services to benefit government, industry, and travelers by undertaking the following:

  – Immediately recognize NEXUS members for trusted traveler lanes at passenger pre-board screening points for flights from Canada to the United States.

  – Jointly develop a plan by June 30, 2012, to incorporate third country traveler programs.

  – Develop program enhancements for all modes in the following areas: enrolment (including mobile enrolment); compliance (e.g., review compliance enforcement and redress); and other benefits within 2 years.

- Include Canadian NEXUS members in a TSA risk-based screening program that provides differential treatment based on risk, upon implementation of such a program. Within 18 months of TSA implementing a risk-based screening program, Canada and the United States will mutually recognize the passenger checkpoint screening measures for those trusted air traveler program members included in the risk-based program. Additionally, we will consider other categories of travelers who could be eligible to participate in the risk-based screening program.

- Extend by June 30, 2012, NEXUS membership eligibility to American and Canadian citizens who currently do not reside in Canada or the United States.

- Develop by June 2012 criteria to extend the applicability of the FAST card for drivers to cover other specified security programs involving U.S. Customs and Border Protection (CBP), CBSA, and other relevant departments and agencies.

Additionally, the United States and Canada will implement a joint marketing campaign to promote trusted traveler programs, implement an "enrolment blitz" at existing centers, and implement an expedited renewal process by March 31, 2012.

Measuring Progress: DHS, CBSA, and Transport Canada will measure and compare wait times between NEXUS and non-NEXUS travelers, percentage of traffic, benefit increase for NEXUS members, and client feedback. With respect to the joint marketing campaign, they will measure membership, use, and satisfaction.

- **Enhance facilities to support trusted trader and traveler programs.**

Next Steps: By March 31, 2012, we will develop a plan to expand NEXUS lanes, booths, and access to the lanes as required, at jointly identified ports of entry to accommodate the expected increase in NEXUS membership as a result of the implementation of the Beyond the Border Action Plan. Additionally, by December 2012, we will conduct a review of the FAST program to determine if future investments are warranted, and at which locations. Wherever feasible, the number of NEXUS lanes and booths will be aligned at each border crossing. As a first step, to align with existing U.S. investments, Canada will, by June 2013, expand NEXUS lanes and booths at the following locations: Abbotsford, B.C.; Aldergrove, B.C.; Douglas, B.C.; Fort Erie, Ontario; Lacolle, Quebec; Pacific Highway, B.C.; Queenston, Ontario; Sarnia, Ontario; and Windsor, Ontario.

This work will be undertaken in coordination with provincial and state agencies.

Measuring Progress: By March 31, 2012, DHS, the U.S. Department of Transportation (DOT), and CBSA will report publicly on a plan toward implementing the new technology at all identified border crossings within the identified timeframes. Additionally, they will report on associated reductions in wait times achieved through these investments.

Develop Additional Initiatives for Expediting Legitimate Travelers and Cargo

- **Implement additional pre-inspection and pre-clearance initiatives.**

  Next Steps: We will develop a comprehensive approach to pre-clearance and pre-inspection covering all modes of cross-border trade and travel. This approach will include the following elements:

  - We will negotiate, by December 2012, a pre-clearance agreement in the land, rail and marine modes to provide the legal framework and reciprocal authorities necessary for the CBP and CBSA to effectively carry out their security, facilitation, and inspection processes in the other country. Concurrently, and as part of those negotiations, the authorities of inspecting officers described in the *Canada–U.S. Air Transport Preclearance Agreement* will be reviewed and amended, on a reciprocal basis, to be comparable to those exercised at airports by officers of the host country.

  - CBSA will conduct full pre-clearance of goods and travelers at Massena, New York. Negotiations to this end will be completed by December 2012.

  - CBP will implement by September 2012 a truck cargo facilitation pilot project in at least one location in Canada to be mutually determined. Based on a positive evaluation of the pilot or pilots, we would consider an expansion to additional sites in both countries.

  - The CFIA and the FSIS will initiate a 1-year pilot by June 2012 to provide for advance review and clearance of official certification and alternative approaches to import inspection activities for fresh meat. The pilot results will be evaluated by September 2013 to inform the future of such work.

  - CBP will conduct full pre-clearance of travelers and accompanying goods at Vancouver, B.C. for passenger rail and cruise ship traffic destined to the United States. Negotiations to this end will be completed by the end of 2012.

  - We will identify and develop solutions to operational impediments to the effectiveness of CBP's pre-clearance operations at Canadian airports by June 2012 (e.g., placement of CATSA screening activities, CBP service levels). Implementation of the agreed solutions will commence in December 2012.

  - We will establish a working group led by APHIS/CBP and CFIA/CBSA to conduct a wood packaging material feasibility study jointly funded by the United States and Canada. The working group will identify and address any policy, program or operational changes required to move inspections for wood packaging material away from the United States–Canada border to the perimeter. This study will be completed by December 2012.

  Measuring Progress: The DHS, FSIS, CFIA, and CBSA will make publicly available the findings from their respective pilots described above and report on reductions in wait times for travelers and cargo and increases in throughput for commercial traffic. We will complete the negotiations on the pre-clearance agreements described above by December 2012.

- **Facilitating the conduct of cross-border business.**

  Next Steps: We will undertake the following:

  - By June 30, 2012, CBP and CBSA will provide enhanced administrative guidance and training to their officers and enhanced operational manuals to achieve optimal operational consistency at all ports of entry on business traveler issues.

  - By June 30, 2012, we will develop and implement operational and administrative policies and requirements to facilitate the movement of specialized personnel to perform maintenance and repairs of industrial machinery and critical operations systems.

  - We will expeditiously pursue changes to existing rules authorizing temporary entry of business visitors who provide after-sale service so they apply equally to those who provide after-lease service as per designated contractual agreements.

  - By August 31, 2012, we will develop and implement specific approaches to incorporate designating documents onto the NEXUS client profile for predictable expedited clearances.

  - We will review current administrative processes under which all categories of business travelers may request adjudication of employment and related petitions by the destination country's immigration authorities to identify and resolve potential issues prior to the actual date of travel. Based on this review, and with the objective of increasing the use of the advanced processes, by September 30, 2012, we will improve current processes and, as appropriate, establish new processes.

  - By June 30, 2012, we will review the effectiveness of existing redress and recourse mechanisms for business travelers whose applications are denied and identify and implement, by December 31, 2012, administrative and operational improvements.

  The U.S. Secretary of Homeland Security and Canada's Minister of Citizenship, Immigration, and Multiculturalism will jointly initiate by March 31, 2012, consultations with stakeholders in both countries. The objective of these consultations will be to identify and assess additional ways to facilitate relevant processes in the near and medium terms through administrative, policy, regulatory, and operational improvements.

  Measuring Progress: A report on the progress on these items and new initiatives will be completed by December 31, 2012. It will be distributed to stakeholders. It will propose options for regular stakeholder engagement and for ongoing improvements for business travelers.

- **Provide a single window through which importers can electronically submit all information to comply with customs and other participating government agency regulations.**

  Next Steps: CBP and CBSA will provide traders with a single window through which they can electronically submit all information required to comply with customs and other government regulations; this information would then be assessed electronically by the relevant government departments and agencies, resulting in border-related decisions which would be transmitted electronically. In doing this, we will:

- Fully implement and align our single-window programs for imports entering our respective countries.

- Convert the data requirements of all participating government departments and agencies to electronic form by 2013. In carrying out this conversion, departments and agencies will review their existing regulatory requirements and identify for conversion only that information which is essential for regulatory purposes.

- As an interim milestone, convert border-related decision processes for at least the top four priority departments and agencies to electronic form no later than December 2013.

Measuring Progress: DHS and CBSA will measure the increased number of participating government agencies conducting business electronically and the number of permits, licences and certificates that are converted from paper to electronic form.

- **Promote supply chain connectivity by harmonizing low-value shipment processes to expedite customs administration.**

  Next Steps: We will increase and harmonize the value thresholds to $2,500 for expedited customs clearance from the current levels of $2,000 for the United States and $1,600 for Canada.

  - Canada will increase the value threshold to $2,500 for exemption from North American Free Trade Agreement Certificate of Origin requirements, thereby aligning it with the current threshold of the United States.

  Measuring Progress: DHS and CBSA will report publicly on our performance in processing low value shipments on the same day they arrive in the United States or Canada.

- **Bring greater public transparency and accountability to the application of border fees and charges, with a view to reducing costs to business and promoting trade competitiveness.**

  Next Steps: We will:

  - Develop for each country an inventory of fees and charges at the border, which sets out their purpose and legal basis, how they are collected, how much is collected, their intended use, and the rationale for collecting them at the border; and

  - Commission a third party to conduct an economic impact assessment of such fees, including their cumulative effect, on the competitive position of three economic sectors in the United States and Canada for which cross-border activity is important.

  Measuring Progress: Based on the above work, DHS and Public Safety Canada will produce and publish a joint "Report on Border Fees," setting out the inventory of fees in each country and the results of the economic impact assessment of the three sectors, which will be made available to the public by September 30, 2012.

Invest in Improving Shared Border Infrastructure and Technology

- **Coordinate border infrastructure investment and upgraded physical infrastructure at key border crossings.**

  Next Steps: We will develop a joint Border Infrastructure Investment Plan to ensure a mutual understanding of available funding for targeted projects and the schedule, scope, and responsibilities for those projects in consultation and coordination with all applicable local, state or provincial, and federal stakeholders.

  We commit to make significant investments in physical infrastructure at key crossings to relieve congestion and speed the movement of traffic across the border. Examples of the significant infrastructure upgrades may include: customs plaza replacement and redevelopment, additional primary inspection lanes and booths, expanded or new secondary inspection facilities, and expanded or new connecting roads, highway interchanges, and bridges.

  As initial respective priorities, the United States will put forward for approval Alexandria Bay, New York; Blue Water Bridge, Michigan; Lewiston Bridge, New York; Peace Bridge, New York for such investments and Canada will put forward Emerson, Manitoba; Lacolle, Quebec; Lansdowne, Ontario; North Portal, Saskatchewan; and Peace Bridge, Ontario.

  By June 30, 2012 we will develop coordinated project investment and implementation plans that will, together with infrastructure-specific actions at small/remote crossings, constitute the first bilateral 5-year Border Infrastructure Investment Plan to be renewed annually.

  Measuring Progress: DOT, DHS, Transport Canada, and CBSA will report progress in a *Border Infrastructure Investment Plan-Progress Report* that outlines specific projects that are planned for future years and investments to date. The report also will describe increased capacity (measured by the number, percentage increase in inspection lanes, and primary inspection booths), the number and percentage increase in secondary inspection bays, increased space for secondary inspections, and the percentage increase in space for secondary inspections and changes in border wait time. Reductions in the environmental impact due to reduced border wait times will be measured in decreases and percentage decreases in tons of greenhouse gas emissions. DOT, CBP, Transport Canada, and CBSA also will report on reductions in wait times at the border.

- **Coordinate plans for physical infrastructure upgrades at small and remote ports of entry.**

  Next Steps: We will better coordinate joint port of entry investment and enhance client service by:

    - Establishing a small and remote port working group to evaluate a binational approach to operational alignment (for example, mirroring hours), infrastructure investment, and improved service;

    - Arriving at consensus recommendations for all small and remote ports to include analyses of hours of operation, technology-only processing solutions, joint or co-managed facilities, and aligned plans for expansions and closures;

- Based upon consensus recommendations, developing joint action plans for implementation, covering the short-, medium-, and long-term objectives; and

- Incorporating binational infrastructure recommendations into the bilateral five-year Border Infrastructure Investment Plan.

Measuring Progress: DOT, DHS, Transport Canada, and CBSA will develop joint action plans for all small ports by June 30, 2012 and incorporate recommendations into the bilateral 5-year Border Infrastructure Investment Plan on an annual basis, beginning June 30, 2012.

- **Implement a border wait-time measurement system at mutually determined high priority United States–Canada border crossings.**

  Next Steps: CBP and CBSA will develop a plan to identify reasonable and achievable border wait time service levels at major crossings. Real time border wait time information will be made available to border and transportation agencies to better manage their resources and to drivers to make informed decisions about when and where to cross the border. This may lead to increased efficiency and reduced delays at the border. Installation of the border wait time measurement system will be completed over the next 3 years at the top 20 crossings. Wait time information will be available on the websites of CBP, DOT, Transport Canada, and CBSA and through other electronic media such as Twitter and the Government of Canada's Wireless Portal.

  Measuring Progress: Wait time service levels at key crossings will be published jointly by DOT, CBP, CBSA, and Transport Canada by June 30, 2012. Real time information will be available to the public on websites, roadside signs, and other traveler information systems by the end of 2013.

- **Facilitate secure passage and expedite processing through implementing Radio Frequency Identification (RFID) technology at appropriate crossings.**

  Next Steps: To align with existing U.S. investments, Canada will deploy RFID technology in a minimum of 2 lanes at 11 land ports: Ambassador Bridge (Windsor, Ontario); Blue Water Bridge (Sarnia, Ontario); Cornwall (Cornwall, Ontario); Douglas (Surrey, B.C.); Emerson (Emerson, Manitoba); Peace Bridge (Fort Erie, Ontario); Lacolle (St-Bernard-de-Lacolle, Quebec); Pacific Highway (Surrey, B.C.); Queenston Bridge (Niagara, Ontario); Rainbow Bridge (Niagara, Ontario); and Windsor-Detroit Tunnel (Windsor, Ontario).

  Measuring Progress: The CBSA will report publicly on progress towards installation at selected crossings and the impact on processing times after installation. Additionally, DHS and CBSA will evaluate the number of travelers using RFID-enabled documents such as Enhanced Drivers Licences, U.S. Passport Cards, and NEXUS cards.

- **Enhance Binational Port Operations Committees.**

  Next Steps: Building on the twenty land border Binational Port Operations Committees established in 2011, we commit to establish additional committees at the eight international airports in Canada that provide U.S. preclearance. Both the existing and new Binational Port Operations Committees will play an important role in improving how we manage travel and trade flows and expedite the processing of travelers and goods. They will involve CBP, CBSA, and other law enforcement and transportation partners.

Measuring Progress: DHS and Public Safety Canada, in coordination with other law enforcement and transportation partners, will establish the new committees by early 2012. Each committee will meet at least four times per year, and develop an action plan by March 31, 2012. Each committee's action plan will include specific initiatives to improve border management and efficiency. A full evaluation of the committees will be conducted by the end of 2012, and the addition of committees at other land ports of entry will be considered in 2013.

Part III: Cross-Border Law Enforcement

The United States and Canada have developed successful models for preventing criminals from crossing the border to escape justice. The Shiprider pilot program, for example, employs cross-designated officers to patrol the maritime areas between our two countries, while Integrated Border Enforcement Teams and Border Enforcement Security Taskforces support joint investigations and law enforcement action at and between ports of entry. The Beyond the Border Action Plan moves forward with new initiatives that build on these successful law enforcement programs.

Deepen Cooperative Investigation and Prosecution Efforts to Identify and Stop Serious Offenders and Violent Criminals

- **Cooperate on national security and transnational criminal investigations.**

  Next Steps: The United States and Canada will develop integrated cross-border law enforcement operations, including deploying regularized Shiprider teams.

  In addition, we will implement two "Next Generation" pilot projects to create integrated teams in areas such as intelligence, criminal investigations, and an intelligence-led uniformed presence between ports of entry. This model draws on the proven cross-border policing approaches that were introduced by Shiprider, while incorporating the best practices and successes of other existing border law enforcement programs such as the Integrated Border Enforcement Teams and the Border Enforcement Security Task Forces.

  Measuring Progress: Canada will pursue the ratification of the Shiprider Framework Agreement by winter 2011–2012 to enable deployment of regularized Shiprider operations with at least two shiprider teams to be deployed by summer 2012 and an additional two teams to be deployed in 2015-2016.

  The DOJ, DHS, the Royal Canadian Mounted Police (RCMP), Public Safety Canada, and Justice Canada will complete the scope of operations and program architecture for the "Next Generation" pilot projects by spring or summer 2012, and two pilots will be deployed simultaneously by summer 2012.

- **Provide interoperable radio capability for law enforcement actors.**

  Next Steps: We will implement a binational radio interoperability system between U.S. and Canadian border enforcement personnel to permit law enforcement agencies to coordinate effective binational investigations and timely responses to border incidents, while improving both officer and public safety.

  Measuring Progress: DOJ, DHS, RCMP, and Public Safety Canada will fully implement this system within 3 years and will measure success through technical means such as system availability and user input and surveys.

Part IV: Critical Infrastructure and Cybersecurity

The United States and Canada are connected by critical infrastructure—from bridges and roads to energy infrastructure and cyberspace. The Beyond the Border Action Plan includes measures to enhance the resiliency of our shared critical and cyber infrastructure, and to enable our two countries to rapidly respond to and recover from disasters and emergencies on either side of the border.

Enhance the Resiliency of our Shared Critical and Cyber Infrastructure

- **Execute programs and develop joint products to enhance cross-border critical infrastructure protection and resilience.**

  Next Steps: We will implement the Canada-United States Action Plan for Critical Infrastructure, including by executing programs and developing joint products to enhance cross-border critical infrastructure protection and resilience. As part of this effort, we will conduct a regional resilience assessment program (RRAP) for the Maine-New Brunswick region, and create binational mechanisms for joint risk analysis, which will share information and develop joint analytic products.

  Measuring Progress: The pilot RRAP will be launched in 2011-2012 and completed by December 31, 2013. We expect that the binational mechanisms for conducting joint risk analysis will be established by June 30, 2012. The U.S. Department of State (DOS), DHS, and Public Safety Canada will report on implementation, including the number of joint or other products used in developing mitigation plans or addressing a capability gap, and the number of training sessions conducted.

- **Protect vital government and critical digital infrastructure of binational importance, and make cyberspace safer for all our citizens.**

  Next Steps: We will enhance our already strong bilateral cyber security cooperation to better protect vital government and critical digital infrastructure and increase both countries' ability to respond jointly and effectively to cyber incidents. This will be achieved through joint projects and operational efforts, including joint briefings with the private sector and other stakeholders and the enhancement of real-time information sharing between operation centers.

  Measuring Progress: DOS, DHS, and Public Safety Canada will report on joint or coordinated engagements with the private sector and external stakeholders, including joint briefings and presentations, assistance provided during the course of a cyber incident, and joint communications products that are developed.

- **Expand joint leadership on international cyber security efforts.**

  Next Steps: We will strengthen cooperation on international cyber security and Internet governance issues to promote prosperity, enhance security, and preserve openness in our networked world. To achieve these goals, we will explore opportunities for improved engagement with third countries and in appropriate multilateral forums. Canada will accede in the coming months to the Council of Europe Convention on Cybercrime and both countries also will explore opportunities to promote the Convention.

  Measuring Progress: DOS and Public Safety Canada will report on the effectiveness of sharing cyber security best practices, the number of engagements with third countries, and how these efforts have translated into advancing American–Canadian objectives on cyber issues in international forums.

Rapidly Respond to and Recover from Disasters and Emergencies on Either Side of the Border

- **Mitigate the impacts of disruptions on communities and the economy by managing traffic in the event of an emergency at affected border crossings.**

  Next Steps—Land crossings: We commit to finalizing a guide that outlines best practices and considerations for border traffic management in the event of an emergency to support planning at individual border crossings. Building on this guide, officials will engage regional partners to support the development of regional cross-border plans and conduct exercises to ensure that these plans would be effective in the event of a disruption.

  Next Steps—Maritime commerce: We commit to collaborate at the regional level between countries to facilitate maritime commerce recovery following an emergency. This will be achieved by developing joint strategies, processes, or plans to facilitate the sharing of information and resources during emergencies, the dissemination of best practices, and the development of clear lines of communication consistent with agreed information elements.

  Measuring Progress: For land border crossings, DOS, DHS, and Public Safety Canada will report annually on the percentage of priority border crossings that are covered by a regional plan and validated through an exercise.

  DOS, DHS, Public Safety Canada, CBSA, and Transport Canada will work in the maritime commerce arena to establish or identify and leverage an existing joint United States-Canadian Pacific Region committee by January 31, 2012; develop preliminary planning guides, communications, and information-sharing protocols by June 30, 2012; conduct a tabletop exercise to validate concepts and mechanisms by October 31, 2012 followed by adjustments to these instruments for use in other regions; report on results of the exercise and finalize a schedule of periodic reviews of concepts and processes in winter 2012–2013; and establish or identify and leverage existing joint United States-Canadian Atlantic and Great Lakes committees by June 30, 2013, followed by implementation of validated plans and procedures.

-

- **Enhance our collective preparedness and response capacity for health security threats.**

  Next Steps: We commit to develop a set of measures to reduce the impacts of shared health security risks. This initiative will be phased in over a period of 2 years, beginning with information sharing to explore how each nation determines health security risk and concluding with an appropriate arrangement that records measures for effective cross-border collaboration. We will enhance preparedness and response capacity through a risk-based approach to planning, which will be supported by appropriate information-, personnel-, and equipment-sharing arrangements and partnerships.

  Measuring Progress: DHS and Public Safety Canada, in coordination with other health partners, will complete this work by summer 2013.

- **Establish binational plans and capabilities for emergency management, with a focus on chemical, biological, radiological, nuclear, and explosives (CBRNE) events.**

  Next Steps: We commit to establishing two new working groups to jointly improve our ability to prepare for and respond to binational disasters. The first working group will focus on preventing, mitigating, preparing for, responding to, and recovering from CBRNE events. It will:

  - Establish joint training opportunities and share lessons learned to enhance preparedness for, and response to, CBRNE events in both countries;

  - Establish bilateral information-exchange opportunities to share advancements in policies, plans, science and technology, and lessons learned;

  - Establish a strategy that can enhance bilateral interoperability for conducting CBRNE response; and

  - Develop a mutual assistance CBRNE concept of operations.

  The second working group will focus on cross-border interoperability as a means of harmonizing cross-border emergency communications efforts. It will pursue activities that promote the harmonization of the Canadian Multi-Agency Situational Awareness System with the United States Integrated Public Alert and Warning System to enable sharing of alert, warning, and incident information to improve response coordination during binational disasters. Specifically, this working group will:

  - Coordinate national-level emergency communications plans and strategies;

  - Identify future trends and technologies related to communications interoperability;

  - Promote the use of standards in emergency communications;

  - Promote governance models and structures; and

  - Share best practices and lessons learned.

  Measuring Progress: DOS, DHS, and Public Safety Canada will establish the working groups that will develop work plans and validation metrics by October 30, 2012. They will validate their bilateral efforts within a five-year period.

Part V: Managing Our New Long-Term Partnership

- **Establish a Beyond the Border Executive Steering Committee to oversee the successful implementation of the Action Plan and maintain transparency and accountability.**

Next Steps: We will form an Assistant Secretary/Assistant Deputy Minister-level Beyond the Border Executive Steering Committee (BTB ESC) that will hold annual meetings to discuss the management of the shared border, progress on identified initiatives, and identify areas of further work.

The first order of business for the BTB ESC will be to oversee the implementation of the Action Plan. To ensure continued transparency and accountability, Canada and the United States will generate a joint, public annual *Beyond the Border Implementation Report*, which will be issued yearly during the 3-year period set out in the Leaders' February 4, 2011 Declaration, with the expectation of continuation.

The report will be submitted to the President of the United States by the Secretary of State in coordination with the Secretary of Homeland Security, the Secretary of Commerce and the Attorney General; and to the Prime Minister of Canada by the Minister of Public Safety and the Minister of International Trade.

Measuring Progress: The first BTB ESC will be convened by June 30, 2012, and the initial *Beyond the Border Implementation Report* will be released by December 31, 2012.

- **Develop a joint statement of joint United States–Canada privacy principles to inform and guide information and intelligence sharing under the Beyond the Border Action Plan.**

Next Steps: Our countries have a long history of sharing information responsibly and respecting our separate constitutional and legal frameworks that protect privacy. Responsible sharing not only demonstrates respect for the rule of law but also facilitates and promotes the flow of accurate, relevant, and necessary information to address threats to national security and conduct law enforcement while respecting citizens' civil liberties. It is in this spirit that the Beyond the Border Declaration commits our two countries to protecting privacy in all the initiatives we are undertaking, and to stating the privacy protection principles that will inform and guide our work in this regard.

Along with other issues to be determined, the joint statement of principles will address the following: data quality; necessity and minimization; access; record ratification; purpose specification and use limitation; onward transfer to third countries; retention; security safeguards; effective oversight; redress and transparency; and appropriate exceptions to these principles, such as exceptions intended to protect the privacy and identity of a victim and the identity of an informant, as well as against disclosure of information that could jeopardize a law enforcement investigation.

Measuring Progress: DHS, DOJ, Public Safety Canada, and Justice Canada will complete the statement by May 30, 2012.

www.ingramcontent.com/pod-product-compliance
Lightning Source LLC
Chambersburg PA
CBHW081805280526
45789CB00008B/3012